Emergency Vehicles

Chris Oxlade

www.heinemann.co.uk
Visit our website to find out more information about Heinemann Library books.

To order:
 Phone 44 (0) 1865 888066
Send a fax to 44 (0) 1865 314091
 Visit the Heinemann Bookshop at www.heinemann.co.uk to browse our catalogue and order online.

First published in Great Britain by Heinemann Library, Halley Court, Jordan Hill, Oxford OX2 8EJ a division of Reed Educational and Professional Publishing Ltd.
Heinemann is a registered trademark of Reed Educational & Professional Publishing Ltd.

OXFORD MELBOURNE AUCKLAND
JOHANNESBURG BLANTYRE GABORONE
IBADAN PORTSMOUTH (NH) USA CHICAGO

Designed by Paul Davies and Associates
Originated by Ambassador Litho Ltd
Printed in Hong Kong/China

05 04 03 02 01
10 9 8 7 6 5 4 3 2 1

ISBN 0431 10854 4

British Library Cataloguing in Publication Data

Oxlade, Chris
Emergency vehicles. – (Transport around the world) 1.Emergency vehicles – Juvenile literature
I.Title
629.2'25

Acknowledgements
The Publishers would like to thank the following for permission to reproduce photographs:
R D Battersby p12; Trevor Clifford pp22, 28; Corbis pp20, 21, 23; Mary Evans Picture Library p9; Eye Ubiquitous pp10, 19; PA Photos p27; Photodisc pp14, 15; Quadrant pp16, 17, 26, 29; Royal Navy p18; Science Museum p8; Shout Picture Library pp4, 5, 6, 7, 11; Tony Stone Images p13; TRH: Canadair pp 24, 25

Cover photograph reproduced with permission of Tony Stone Images

Every effort has been made to contact copyright holders of any material reproduced in this book. Any omissions will be rectified in subsequent printings if notice is given to the Publisher.

Contents

Any words appearing in the text in bold, **like this**, are explained in the glossary.

What is an emergency vehicle?

An emergency vehicle rushes to an accident to help **rescue** people. Cars, trucks, planes and boats can all be emergency vehicles. They have special **equipment** that helps with the rescue.

4

Emergency vehicles have a **crew** who drive the vehicle and work its equipment. The crew of this fire engine are cutting open a car to rescue the driver.

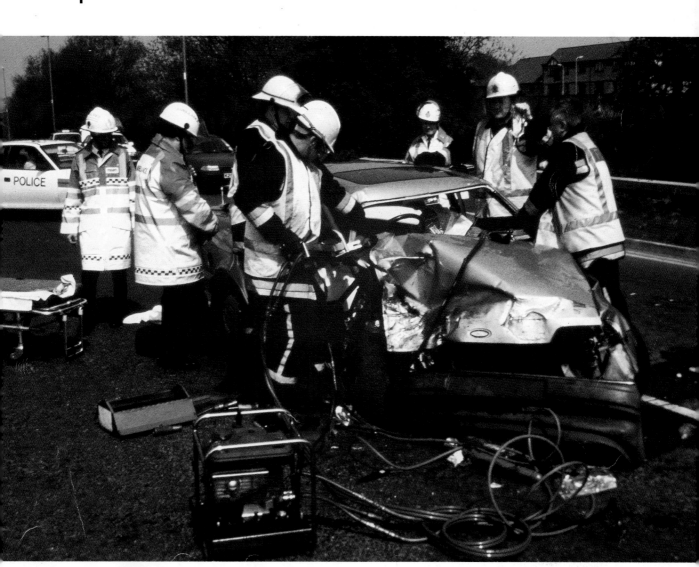

Special parts

In the **cab** of an emergency vehicle there is a **two-way radio**. Using the radio, the **crew** can talk to a control centre. People at the control centre tell the crew where the emergencies are.

Some emergency vehicles have bright floodlights that light up the scene of an emergency at night. They also have flashing lights and loud **sirens** so that people know when they are coming.

Old emergency vehicles

This is an old fire **engine**. It was built in 1866 and was pulled along by horses. Its **crew pumped** water to the fire by moving handles up and down.

Old lifeboats did not have engines. The crew had to row hard to get out to sea. In those days being in a lifeboat crew was a very dangerous job.

Where are emergency vehicles used?

Police **patrol** cars, ambulances and fire **engines** travel on roads. They often have to rush through busy traffic. The driver needs to be skilled and careful.

Some emergency vehicles such as this helicopter fly through the air. They can reach places where there are no roads. **Rescue** boats travel on water to reach people who need help.

Police patrol cars

Police officers **patrol** the streets of towns and cities in patrol cars. Some patrol cars have powerful **engines** so that the officers can reach the accident quickly.

The police officers hear about an emergency on their **two-way radio**. They switch on the patrol car's flashing lights and **sirens** so that other drivers can get out of the way.

Ambulances

An ambulance is a vehicle that carries ill or injured people to hospital. Inside the ambulance there is space to put a person on a **stretcher**.

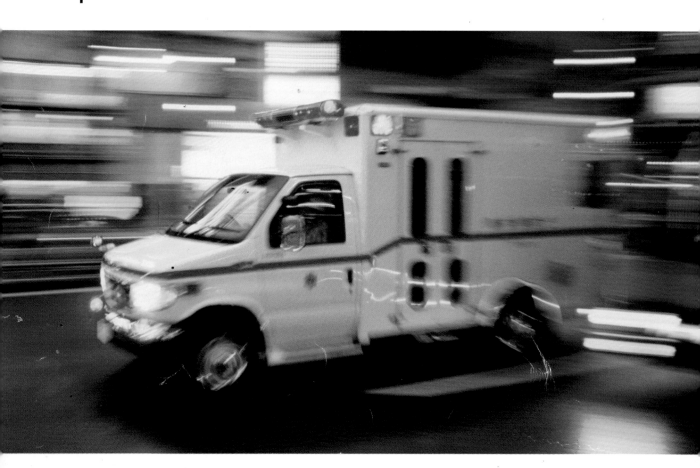

The ambulance **crew** are trained to do **first aid** as well as drive the ambulance. They treat the injured person using first-aid **equipment** as the ambulance travels to hospital.

Flying doctors

In Australia, many people live in remote areas called the outback. Ambulances cannot reach them quickly. The Flying Doctor Service uses special planes that fly people to hospital.

On board the planes are beds for
patients. There is also lots of **equipment**
that doctors can use to treat the
patients as the plane flies along.

Helicopters

This is an air-sea **rescue** helicopter. It rescues people who are in trouble at sea or in the mountains. A helicopter is lifted into the air by its spinning **rotor**.

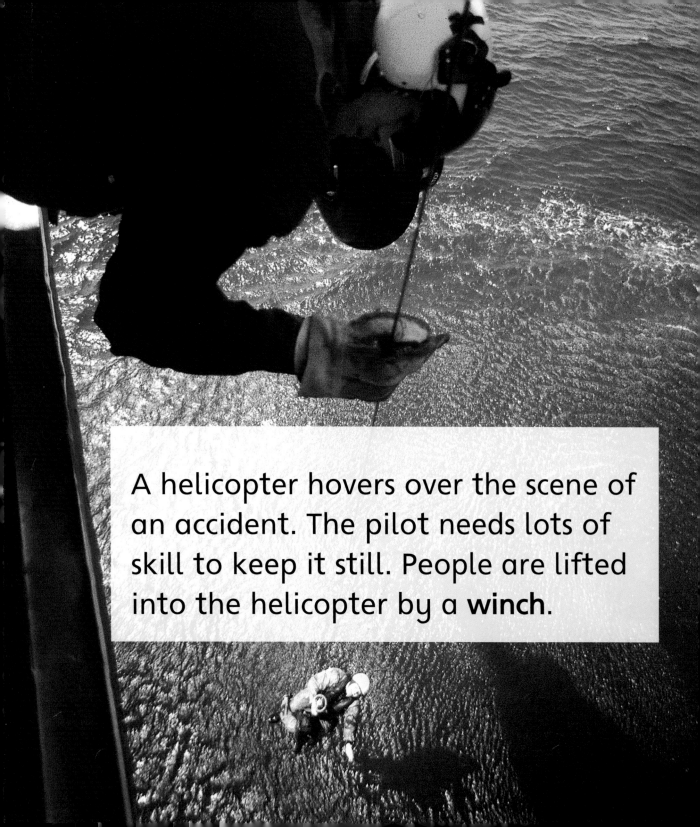

A helicopter hovers over the scene of an accident. The pilot needs lots of skill to keep it still. People are lifted into the helicopter by a **winch**.

Lifeboats

A lifeboat is a boat that **rescues** people from sinking boats and ships. Lifeboats are fast and strong. They can go safely through enormous waves.

A lifeboat must get to sea as quickly as possible when its **crew** get an emergency call. This lifeboat slides down a steep ramp straight into the waves.

Fire engines

ladders

hoses

A fire **engine** is a vehicle that helps to put out fires. It carries lots of fire-fighting **equipment**, such as long ladders and water hoses.

Some fire engines have a huge **tank** of water and a powerful water **pump**. Strong hoses can carry water from the pump or water pipe to the fire.

Water bombers

Some special fire-fighting aircraft drop water on to a forest fire. Normal fire **engines** could not get to the fire through the thick forest.

This fire-fighting aircraft has a big water tank inside. The pilot fills it by skimming over a lake and scooping up water.

Airport fire engines

Every airport has its own fire **engines** like this one. The engines are always ready to rush to the **rescue** in case a plane has an accident.

An airport fire engine has a spray gun on the roof. The gun sprays thick foam like washing-up suds over a crashed plane to stop fire spreading.

Breakdown trucks

A breakdown truck goes to **rescue** cars, trucks and buses that have broken down. A **mechanic** often uses the truck's tools to repair the broken vehicle.

If a vehicle cannot be repaired it is put on the back of the truck to be taken to a garage. A **winch** pulls the car up a ramp at the back of the truck.

Timeline

1800s Fire **engines** are pulled by horses or firemen. Their pumps are worked by firemen using their hands or feet.

1824 The world's first lifeboat service is started in the UK. It uses self-righting lifeboats that were rowed to sea by the **crew**.

1850s The first ambulances are used during the Crimean War. They are horse-drawn carts with stretchers on top.

1885 The first proper car is built in Germany by Karl Benz. It has three wheels and is driven along by a petrol engine. Top speed is 13 kilometres per hour.

1928 In Australia, the Royal Flying Doctor Service is started. It carries doctors to remote towns in the Australian outback.

1940 The first successful helicopter makes a flight. It is the Sikorsky VS-300, designed by Igor Sikorsky.

1967 The Canadair CL-215 water bomber makes its first flight in Canada. It is designed to drop water on forest fires.

Glossary

cab the space at the front of a van or truck where the driver sits

crew group of people working together

engine a machine that powers movement using fuel

equipment machines and supplies that help people do a job

first aid helping someone who is injured, before they get to hospital

mechanic a person who repairs vehicles and their engines

patrol to travel around a town or city looking for emergencies

pump a machine that moves water

rescue to save from danger

rotor blade on a helicopter that spins round

siren a device that makes a loud warning noise

stretcher a simple bed for ill or injured people that can be carried by two people

tank large container for storing something, such as water

two-way radio radio that lets you talk and listen to someone else

winch a machine like the reel on a fishing rod that pulls in cable or rope with an engine or motor

Index

Titles in the *Transport Around The World* series

Hardback   0 431 10840 4

Hardback   0 431 10841 2

Hardback   0 431 10839 0

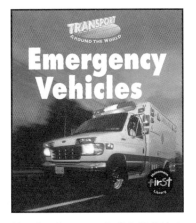

Hardback   0 431 10854 4

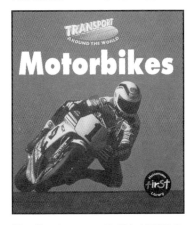

Hardback   0 431 10852 8

Hardback   0 431 10838 2

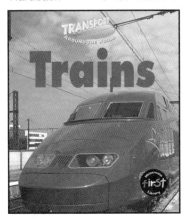

Hardback   0 431 10853 6

Hardback   0 431 10855 2

Find out about the other titles in this series on our website www.heinemann.co.uk/library